Helicopters
on the Go

by Beth Bence Reinke

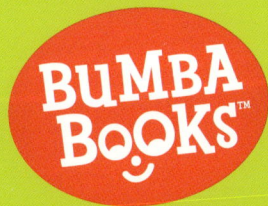

BUMBA BOOKS™

LERNER PUBLICATIONS ◆ MINNEAPOLIS

Note to Educators:

Throughout this book, you'll find critical thinking questions. These can be used to engage young readers in thinking critically about the topic and in using the text and photos to do so.

Lerner Publications Company
A division of Lerner Publishing Group, Inc.
241 First Avenue North
Minneapolis, MN 55401 USA

For reading levels and more information, look up this title at www.lernerbooks.com.

Library of Congress Cataloging-in-Publication Data

The Cataloging-in-Publication Data for *Helicopters on the Go* is on file at the Library of Congress.
978-1-5124-8254-6 (lib. bdg.)
978-1-5415-1114-9 (pbk.)
978-1-5124-8258-4 (EB pdf)

Manufactured in the United States of America
1 – CG – 12/31/17

LERNER
e
SOURCE

Expand learning beyond the printed book. Download free, complementary educational resources for this book from our website, www.lernersource.com.

Table of
Contents

Helicopters 4

Parts of a Helicopter 22

Picture Glossary 23

Read More 24

Index 24

Helicopters

Helicopters are a type

of aircraft.

They fly in the air.

Helicopters do not have wings. Instead, they have rotor blades on top. The blades spin around fast. They lift the helicopter.

Why do you think helicopter blades need to spin fast?

Helicopters fly many ways.

They go forward and backward.

They move up and down.

They can fly sideways too!

Why might a helicopter need to fly sideways?

They can even hover.

The tail rotor has

small blades.

It keeps the helicopter

steady.

The pilot sits in the cockpit.

She flies the helicopter.

Helicopters do many jobs.

This helicopter dumps water on a fire.

Police officers can work

from helicopters.

They search for people

or things from up high.

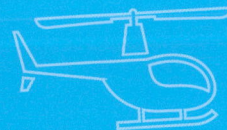

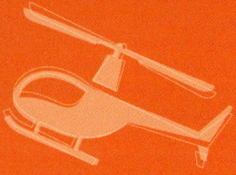

Other helicopters help people.

They fly them to the hospital.

How else could helicopters be used to help people?

The pilot lowers the helicopter.

It lands on skids.

Would you like to ride in a helicopter?

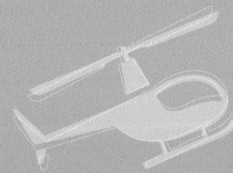

Parts of a Helicopter

rotor blades

tail rotor

cockpit

skids

Picture Glossary

aircraft

a vehicle that travels in the air

cockpit

where the pilot sits in the front of the helicopter

hover

to hang in the air in one place

rotor blades

blades that rotate to lift a helicopter

Read More

Boothroyd, Jennifer. *How Do Helicopters Work?* Minneapolis: Lerner Publications, 2013.

Pettiford, Rebecca. *Helicopters*. Minneapolis: Bellwether Media, 2018.

West, David. *Helicopters*. Mankato, MN: Smart Apple Media, 2016.

Index

cockpit, 13

hover, 10

pilot, 13, 21

rotor blades, 7

skids, 21

tail rotor, 10

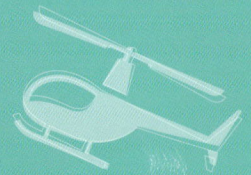

Photo Credits